# A LITTLE BIT OF
# SABRINA CARPENTER

**AN UNOFFICIAL CELEBRATION OF A GLOBAL POP SENSATION**

summersdale

A LITTLE BIT OF SABRINA CARPENTER

Copyright © Octopus Publishing Group Limited, 2025

All rights reserved.

Text by Emily Campbell

No part of this book may be reproduced by any means, nor transmitted, nor translated into a machine language, without the written permission of the publishers.

Condition of Sale
This book is sold subject to the condition that it shall not, by way of trade or otherwise, be lent, resold, hired out or otherwise circulated in any form of binding or cover other than that in which it is published and without a similar condition including this condition being imposed on the subsequent purchaser.

An Hachette UK Company
www.hachette.co.uk

Summersdale Publishers
Part of Octopus Publishing Group Limited
Carmelite House
50 Victoria Embankment
LONDON
EC4Y 0DZ
UK

www.summersdale.com

The authorized representative in the EEA is Hachette Ireland, 8 Castlecourt Centre, Dublin 15, D15 XTP3, Ireland
(email: info@hbgi.ie)

Printed and bound in Poland

ISBN: 978-1-83799-883-8
eISBN: 978-1-83799-884-5

This FSC® label means that materials and other controlled sources used for the product have been responsibly sourced

MIX
Paper | Supporting responsible forestry
FSC® C018236

Substantial discounts on bulk quantities of Summersdale books are available to corporations, professional associations and other organizations. For details contact general enquiries: telephone: +44 (0) 1243 771107 or email: enquiries@summersdale.com.

This book is unofficial and is not endorsed by or in any other way connected with Sabrina Carpenter. Every effort has been made to ensure that all information is correct. Should there be any errors, we apologize and shall be pleased to make the appropriate amendments in any future editions.

TO

..................................................

FROM

..................................................

# INTRODUCTION

Dear reader,

Whether you have been a die-hard fan of Sabrina Carpenter since her Disney Channel days or when you first saw her on the Coachella stage, or you're a recent listener of her *Short n' Sweet* album, this pocket-sized companion is perfect for you.

It's jam-packed with pieces of advice from Sabrina on how to follow her no-nonsense approach to life, facts to leave you with no words, and trivia to test if you really know everything about this busy woman. So, be prepared to brush up on your Sabrina knowledge and see if you really are the sharpest tool!

*A Little Bit of Sabrina Carpenter* is a homage to the pop powerhouse's chart-topping songs, blonde, bouncy blowout and sensational style. It's for all you Carpenters out there – her dedicated community – whether you're a new fan or have supported her from the very beginning.

Read on to discover more about the red lipstick print Sabrina is leaving on pop history!

# THE NUMBER ONE PRIORITY IN LIFE

# IS TO TAKE CARE OF YOURSELF AND MAKE SURE YOU'RE HAPPY.

SABRINA CARPENTER

# DID YOU KNOW...

Perhaps Sabrina was always destined to be a star. Around the age of ten, encouraged by her dad, David Carpenter, she started a YouTube channel where she would share videos of herself singing covers of her favourite songs, including tracks from artists such as Adele and Christina Aguilera.

Sabrina Carpenter hasn't always been a popstar. When she starred in the Disney Channel series *Girl Meets World*, what was her character's name?

---

a) Maya Hart

b) Maya Part

c) Maya Dart

I'VE NEVER PAID TOO MUCH ATTENTION TO WHAT OTHER PEOPLE HAVE SAID OR TO WHAT OTHER PEOPLE HAVE TRIED TO MAKE ME BE. I'VE ALWAYS JUST TRIED TO BE MYSELF.

SABRINA CARPENTER

# DID YOU KNOW...

Sabrina competed in the "Are You a Superstar?" contest organized by the Miley Cyrus Fan Club when she was just ten years old. She did a rendition of her icon Miley's song "Hoedown Throwdown" and placed third overall in the competition, out of 7,000 contestants! Her prize was tickets to Miley's tour in Philadelphia and a meet and greet. Any young Smiler's dream!

What was Sabrina's debut single called?

---

a) "Eyes Wide Open"

b) "Can't Blame a Girl for Trying"

c) "Best Thing I Got"

*It always feels good to put something you're proud of out in the world.*

SABRINA CARPENTER

# DID YOU KNOW...

At the age of just 12, Sabrina appeared in one episode of the American TV series *Orange Is the New Black* as mean girl Jessica Wedge. She may have only appeared in it briefly, but what a cool show to add to her credits!

Which famous popstar revealed they sang "Espresso" non-stop and said, "that song is my jam," when it was released by Sabrina?

---

a) Charli XCX

b) Adele

c) Billie Eilish

**I MIGHT NOT KNOW WHO I WAS YESTERDAY**

**OR WHO I'M GOING TO BE TOMORROW, BUT I KNOW WHO I AM RIGHT NOW.**

SABRINA CARPENTER

# DID YOU KNOW...

The character of Bart Simpson in *The Simpsons* is voiced by Sabrina's aunt – it really is a small world in the entertainment industry! Nancy Cartwright voices some of the other characters too, including Maggie Simpson and Nelson Muntz. Maybe Sabrina took inspiration from her famous aunt's acting career!

Which of these musicals did Sabrina star in at the August Wilson Theatre on Broadway for just two performances before it closed due to the COVID-19 pandemic?

---

a) *Six*

b) *& Juliet*

c) *Mean Girls*

THINGS HAPPEN
AND THINGS GO
WRONG, AND
YOU JUST SORT
OF DEAL WITH IT
ALONG THE WAY.

SABRINA CARPENTER

# DID YOU KNOW...

Sabrina thought of the idea for her catchy single "Espresso" when she was staying in the village of Chailland, just south of Paris, during her emails i can't send tour. She visited the creperie down the road and ordered a shot of espresso and some champagne – and the concept for the song "Espresso" was born! The instant hit of caffeine from an espresso is compared to a love addiction in the track.

Which film character's name has Sabrina previously used to check into hotel rooms to avoid the paparazzi and also to make the hotel staff laugh?

---

a) Elle Woods
(*Legally Blonde*)

b) Mrs. Doubtfire
(*Mrs. Doubtfire*)

c) Morticia Addams
(*The Addams Family*)

I live every day, day to day. I will go wherever life takes me. I'm not questioning it.

SABRINA CARPENTER

# DID YOU KNOW...

On her emails i can't send tour in 2022, Sabrina added a unique outro to the song "Nonsense" for every one of the 80 cities in which she performed. Atlanta was the first city to experience this personalized city outro. She also did it for the 25 dates she opened for Taylor Swift on her Eras Tour. This innovation left fans eagerly waiting to see what she would add to their city's rendition.

Who collaborated with Sabrina on an additional version of "Please Please Please"?

---

a) Dolly Parton

b) Shania Twain

c) Miley Cyrus

# YOU NEED TO EXPERIENCE LIFE TO BE ABLE TO WRITE ABOUT

# FRIENDSHIPS, RELATIONSHIPS AND HEARTBREAK.

SABRINA CARPENTER

# DID YOU KNOW...

The "Feather" music video caused controversy when it was filmed in a church in New York. The priest – Monsignor Jamie Gigantiello – didn't follow protocol on filming in the church and the video was considered provocative, particularly in its featuring of a crucifix with profanity printed on it and Sabrina dancing on the altar in a short, black dress.

Sabrina was rumoured to be in a love triangle with Joshua Bassett and another famous pop singer. Which single by the other singer allegedly has a reference to Sabrina's part in this?

---

a) "drivers license" by Olivia Rodrigo

b) "Dive" by Olivia Dean

c) "I miss you, I'm sorry" by Gracie Abrams

I'VE ALWAYS JUST
BEEN VERY DRIVEN.
SOME PEOPLE
LIKE TO CALL
IT STUBBORN.
I LIKE TO
SAY DRIVEN.

SABRINA CARPENTER

# DID YOU KNOW...

To celebrate the one-year anniversary of the smash-hit song "Espresso", Sabrina released a new exclusive vinyl of the single with only 1,000 copies available. What made this unique was that the clear vinyl disc had been pressed with a coffee-stain effect to emulate the song's title!

In which US state is Sabrina's hometown?

———

a) Pennsylvania

b) Texas

c) Chicago

*My advice to my younger self is: don't take other people's opinions more seriously than your own.*

SABRINA CARPENTER

# DID YOU KNOW...

In 2017, Sabrina's former music managers Stan Rogow and Elliot Lurie took her to court for allegedly not paying them their commissions after they were fired. The pair were brought on board to elevate Sabrina's status in the music industry alongside her existing manager. They argued that they helped her get her role in *Girl Meets World* and her five-album record deal. They lost the case, but it disrupted Sabrina's career at the time.

What is the name of the song on Sabrina's *Short n' Sweet* album that references the 2007 film starring Elliot Page?

---

a) "James"
b) "Juliet"
c) "Juno"

**IF YOU HAVE SOME SORT OF**

**KNOWLEDGE OR POWER, SHARE [IT] WITH THE WORLD.**

SABRINA CARPENTER

# DID YOU KNOW...

*Short n' Sweet* is Sabrina's sixth studio album but the first one to secure her a singer's dream – a Grammy award. In fact, she won not just Best Pop Vocal Album for *Short n' Sweet* but also Best Pop Solo Performance for "Espresso" at the 2025 Grammys!

Which of Sabrina's music videos does her ex-boyfriend and *Saltburn* star Barry Keoghan feature in?

———

a) "Bed Chem"

b) "15 Minutes"

c) "Please Please Please"

SO MANY PEOPLE
HAVE DEALT WITH
BEING LABELLED
SOMETHING THAT
THEY'RE NOT.

SABRINA CARPENTER

# DID YOU KNOW...

Sabrina counts on ice baths to relieve any post-show aches and pains. She loves to share behind-the-scenes moments with her Carpenter community through Instagram posts, and in 2024 posted a photo showing her in an ice bath – not just filled with icy cold water but with actual ice cubes in it. The Carpenters noted how calm she looked despite being submerged in ice!

On which TV show did Sabrina get her first acting job in 2011?

———

a) *This Is Who I Am*

b) *Law and Order: Special Victims Unit*

c) *Tall Girl*

I think everybody deserves a fresh start.

SABRINA CARPENTER

# DID YOU KNOW...

Sabrina is a busy woman with many talents! As well as singing, song writing and appearing in films and TV shows, she has also voiced characters for several animated series. Most significantly, she was the voice talent for Princess Vivian in *Sophia the First* and Nina Glitter in *Mickey and the Roadster Racers*, plus various characters in *Phineas and Ferb*.

Which pop superstar asked Sabrina to join her on tour after the success of Sabrina's Radio Disney Music Award-nominated single "Why"?

---

a) Katy Perry

b) Selena Gomez

c) Ariana Grande

# THE MORE I KEEP CREATING,

# THE MORE IDEAS JUST COME OUT OF THE WOODWORK.

SABRINA CARPENTER

# DID YOU KNOW...

Sabrina teased the identity of the actor playing a key role in her "Taste" music video by posting a picture showing the backs of her and another woman in black dresses. It was later revealed that Jenna Ortega was the other woman. Inspired by the 1992 film *Death Becomes Her* and other cult classics, the rather gory video, directed by Dave Meyers, comes with a prewarning for viewers. Sabrina and Jenna play arch enemies violently fighting over a man.

> YOU END UP FINDING WHAT MAKES YOU FEEL COMFORTABLE. FOR ME, CLOTHING HAS HAD A HUGE PART IN THAT.

SABRINA CARPENTER

Which label did Sabrina originally sign to at the age of 14 with a five-album record deal?

———————

a) Hollywood Records

b) Island Records

c) Polydor Records

*Everybody has their own story — it's who you are.*

SABRINA CARPENTER

# DID YOU KNOW...

In 2024, Sabrina made it onto *TIME* magazine's annual "100 Next" list, which features the top 100 up-and-coming leaders across all industries around the world who are shaping our collective future. Sabrina was on the front cover of *TIME*'s special edition for the list and performed at the celebratory party. Quite the leading lady!

What is Sabrina's middle name?

———

a) Anna
b) Annabelle
c) Annlynn

I COULDN'T REALLY PICTURE A

WORLD WITHOUT MUSIC. IT WOULD BE QUITE BORING.

SABRINA CARPENTER

# DID YOU KNOW...

Sabrina is known for sharing her heartbreak advice and tips online. She once told her fans on TikTok that, when you are midway through doing a full face of makeup and feel like you are going to cry, you should tilt your head forward to avoid tears directly going on your makeup. Sabrina's got your back when it comes to practical ways of dealing with the highs and lows of life!

Which type of vehicle is Sabrina driving at the start of the "Espresso" music video?

---

a) A boat

b) A motorbike

c) A tuk-tuk

EVERYONE TAKES
A BAD SELFIE –
THE FIRST THING
IS TO KNOW THAT.

SABRINA CARPENTER

# DID YOU KNOW...

When Sabrina rejoined Taylor Swift on her Eras Tour for the Latin American leg, she decided she would do her very own rendition of one of Taylor's songs. She recorded a country-style, slowed down and ethereal version of "I Knew You Were Trouble" for Spotify. It sounds like a completely different song in Sabrina's own unique style and is a perfect ode to Taylor.

Which of Sabrina's songs is said to express her frustrations at the misogynistic backlash she received when dating Joshua Bassett?

---

a) "Vicious"

b) "because i liked a boy"

c) "Nonsense"

Time will heal everything.

SABRINA CARPENTER

# DID YOU KNOW...

Sabrina donated some of her iconic dresses to a Los Angeles wildfires charity auction as part of the Give a Frock campaign alongside other singers including Chappell Roan. Sabrina's donations included the polka-dot outfit she wore in the "Taste" music video and the blue velvet mini dress from the "Please Please Please" video. The two pieces raised $57,150 (around £43,000) for charity through the auction.

Sabrina got her first dog when she was 13, and it was nominated for the 2019 iHeartRadio Music Award for Cutest Musician's Pet. What is its name?

———

a) Gizmo

b) Goldie

c) Goodwin

# YOUR RELATIONSHIP WITH YOURSELF

## IS GOING TO TAKE YOU THROUGH THE REST OF YOUR LIFE.

SABRINA CARPENTER

# DID YOU KNOW...

Sabrina says *Short n' Sweet* feels like a self-titled album to her: "It's sort of like Sabrina in another language to me." The feelings of fun and forwardness that make up Sabrina's own personality are reflected in the songs on the album.

What does influencer and YouTube star Emma Chamberlain playfully call Sabrina?

———

a) Sab Carp

b) Rina

c) Saffy C

> MUSIC IS WHERE I STARTED. IT'S KIND OF THE BASE OF EVERYTHING.
>
> — SABRINA CARPENTER

# DID YOU KNOW...

"Espresso" was one of the fastest tracks to reach 2 billion streams on Spotify, and it made it to number one on the global Spotify chart too. Sabrina also became the first artist since the Beatles to have two songs debut in the Billboard Hot 100. She's making pop history!

Which of these foods is Sabrina not allergic to?

———

a) Apples
b) Almonds
c) Avocados

*You're born to be who you are.*

SABRINA CARPENTER

# DID YOU KNOW...

Sabrina lives by writing things down. As part of her songwriting process, she records all her thoughts in a notebook or as a voice note, regardless of whether they feel necessary. She finds all these little thoughts guide her to the songs she really wants to write.

Which film character did Sabrina dress like at the premiere of *Horns* in 2014?

---

**a) Alice**
from *Alice in Wonderland*

**b) Belle**
from *Beauty and the Beast*

**c) Dorothy**
from *The Wizard of Oz*

# BE PASSIONATE

## ABOUT EVERYTHING YOU DO.

SABRINA CARPENTER

# DID YOU KNOW...

When Sabrina released her perfume range, the first, signature scent Sweet Tooth, was reported to have sold a bottle every 2 minutes in the UK! The bottle is shaped like a chocolate bar, and there are now three other scents too. Sabrina says Caramel Dream is the fragrance that makes her feel most confident.

What are Sabrina's sisters called?

———

a) Shannon, Sam and Chloe

b) Sarah, Shannon and Cayla

c) Scarlett, Sarah and Sophia

I GET INSPIRATION FROM LITERALLY EVERYTHING AND ANYTHING.

SABRINA CARPENTER

# DID YOU KNOW...

During every performance of her Short n' Sweet tour, Sabrina drank a "Sabrina Extra" beer and played spin the bottle to pick a surprise song. The songs were mainly covers – she put her red lipstick stamp on everything from "Mamma Mia" by ABBA to "That Don't Impress Me Much" by Shania Twain. However, in Philadelphia she had the bottle fall on the bonus track "Busy Woman" from the deluxe album *Short n' Sweet(er)*.

Which of these Sabrina album titles is not also the title of the album's first track?

---

a) *emails i can't send*

b) *EVOLution*

c) *Eyes Wide Open*

*Singing is about telling a story.*

SABRINA CARPENTER

# DID YOU KNOW...

Sabrina has five tattoos! They are quite small and discreet, but each one has its own unique meaning. Sabrina got her first one when she was 21 years old, and it's the word "lucky" on the back of her neck – the name of her childhood teddy and a feeling to which she relates. She also has a heart behind her ear, a butterfly on her ribcage, the phrase "at last" on her left shoulder and the title of her album *Short n' Sweet* on her right one.

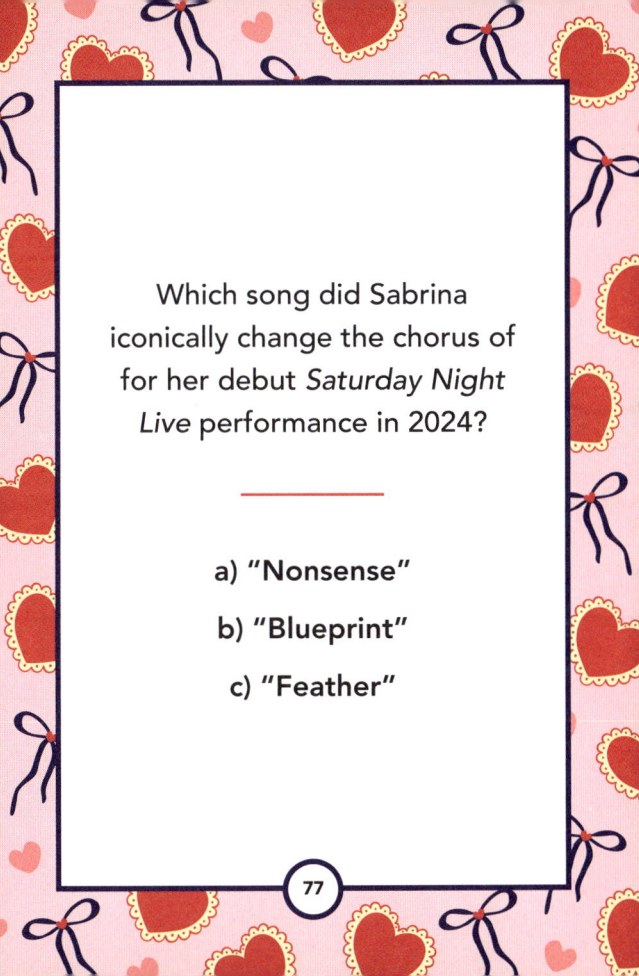

Which song did Sabrina iconically change the chorus of for her debut *Saturday Night Live* performance in 2024?

---

a) "Nonsense"

b) "Blueprint"

c) "Feather"

# WHAT YOU WEAR ONSTAGE IS

# A REFLECTION OF YOUR ARTISTRY.

SABRINA CARPENTER

# DID YOU KNOW...

Sabrina really knows how to make her mark on the entertainment industry. As well as playing the lead role of Quinn Ackerman in the 2020 film *Work It*, she was also one of its executive producers. On this job, she found herself among singing royalty as pop legend Alicia Keys also helped produce the film.

Which of these isn't a part of Sabrina's signature look?

———

a) A fresh, bouncy blowout
b) A long, floaty dress
c) Rosy, dewy makeup

MISTAKES LEAD
YOU TO KNOWING
YOURSELF
THE MOST.

SABRINA CARPENTER

# DID YOU KNOW...

On her Short n' Sweet tour, Sabrina wore pairs of tights that had different lines of writing on the thigh like a tattoo. The words were usually lyrics from one of her songs, and fans waited in anticipation to see what would be featured on the tights on their tour date. She wore tights with lines from the tracks "Juno", "Nonsense", "Espresso" and many more.

Which colour is the front cover of Sabrina's *EVOLution* album?

---

a) Brown

b) Yellow

c) Green

*Your own instincts are your best friend.*

SABRINA CARPENTER

# DID YOU KNOW...

Sabrina made a guest appearance in an episode of *Austin & Ally* on the Disney Channel in 2013 – this was in fact a year before she became a cast regular on *Girl Meets World*. The episode of *Austin & Ally* she featured in is called "Moon Week & Mentors"; Sabrina stars as Lucy, who takes part in a singing competition judged by Austin and Ally.

Who was Sabrina's first celebrity crush?

---

**a) Zac Efron**

**b) Nick Jonas**

**c) Corbin Bleu**

# I'M A MESS IF I DON'T WEAR

# THINGS I FEEL CONFIDENT IN.

SABRINA CARPENTER

# DID YOU KNOW...

On her Short n' Sweet tour before singing "Taste", Sabrina would walk onstage wrapped in a towel with rhinestones on the inside. She would open the towel to reveal her sparkly bodysuit underneath. In London, the towel was decorated with a rhinestoned Union Jack flag. In Los Angeles in November 2024, the towel read "Coming Soon" in glittery writing, which led fans to speculate what was coming next.

Which singer has said he would love to collaborate on a song with Sabrina? (Sabrina has also said she'd love to make a "fun" song with him too!)

---

a) Conan Gray

b) Troye Sivan

c) Charlie Puth

> THE MORE I'M HONEST WITH MYSELF, THE MORE OTHER PEOPLE FEEL LIKE IT FORCES THEM TO BE HONEST AS WELL.
>
> SABRINA CARPENTER

# DID YOU KNOW...

Sabrina is a massive fan of legendary Swedish pop group ABBA. She even named her cats Benny and Björn after the two male members of the group, Björn Ulvaeus and Benny Andersson! After covering "Mamma Mia" on her Short n' Sweet tour, she caught the attention of movie star Amanda Seyfried, who plays Sophie in the *Mamma Mia!* films. Amanda said in an interview she would love Sabrina to play her daughter in the next film!

What is on the front cover of Sabrina's album *Singular: Act I*?

———

a) Sabrina next to a taxi

b) Sabrina in an elevator

c) Sabrina on an escalator

I think it's okay to be confident one day and really insecure the next.

SABRINA CARPENTER

# DID YOU KNOW...

Sabrina has never eaten from the fast-food chain McDonald's! She said she wants to complete a goal before she indulges in one of their burgers to celebrate. Fans have speculated that this goal could be her winning a Grammy, and when she won two in 2025 they waited in anticipation for her to try her first McDonald's meal. To date, there's been no confirmation from Sabrina on whether she has!

What is Sabrina's star sign?

———

**a) Virgo**

**b) Leo**

**c) Taurus**

# BEING BODY POSITIVE

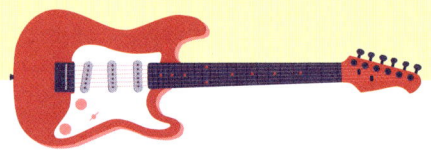

## IS REALLY IMPORTANT TO YOUR OVERALL HAPPINESS.

SABRINA CARPENTER

# DID YOU KNOW...

"Taste" is allegedly about Sabrina and Shawn Mendes's brief relationship in 2023. In March of that year, Shawn and Sabrina were seen leaving Miley Cyrus's album-release party together, and it was speculated they were seeing each other. However, it is said that Shawn quickly went back to former flame Camila Cabello. In "Taste", Sabrina seems to tell Camila to be careful.

Who was Sabrina's first public boyfriend?

---

a) Bradley Steven Perry
b) Peyton Meyer
c) Joshua Bassett

THE PEOPLE THAT
DO LIKE YOU AND
DO SUPPORT YOU
AND LOVE YOU –
THOSE ARE THE
PEOPLE TO FOCUS
ON, AND THAT'S
ALL THAT MATTERS.

SABRINA CARPENTER

# DID YOU KNOW...

Sabrina has said that her favourite dish is chicken fajitas, and she has credited her dad with teaching her how to make them. For a pre-event snack, she likes hummus with pitta bread and vegetable sticks – or crudités as she refers to them. She also loves fries!

Which of these items is essential to Sabrina when she is on tour?

———

a) A vocal steamer

b) A blanket

c) A mini fridge

I have to find the joy in life because I know that it's out there, because if I found it once I can find it again.

SABRINA CARPENTER

# DID YOU KNOW...

During the recording of *Short n' Sweet*, Sabrina surprised herself at how high her vocal range can go. The harmonies are stacked together on the album, making it feel full of life. Sabrina says the harmonies in the background of *Short n' Sweet* are just as important as the lead vocals.

Which of these fashion trends does Sabrina Carpenter wish would return?

---

a) Chokers

b) Leg warmers

c) Heelys

**NO MATTER HOW MUCH I EXPERIENCE,**

**I WILL ALWAYS HAVE SOMETHING TO LEARN.**

SABRINA CARPENTER

# DID YOU KNOW...

The Beatles inspired Sabrina to start writing her own music. When she was young, her dad played their track "Rocky Raccoon" to her, and she was mesmerized both by the songwriting and by Paul McCartney. She eventually got to meet Paul and has said that she admires how he makes everyone he meets feel seen and heard.

Which song has Sabrina said is the most personal on her *Short n' Sweet* album?

———

a) "Lie To Girls"
b) "Slim Pickins"
c) "Dumb & Poetic"

> I THINK SOMETHING HAPPENS WHEN YOU GET TO A CERTAIN POINT IN YOUR LIFE WHERE YOU JUST KIND OF STOP CARING AND YOU JUST START LIVING.
>
> SABRINA CARPENTER

# DID YOU KNOW...

Sabrina has spoken about the misconception that she doesn't write her own songs because she works with producers and cowriters. In actual fact, she cowrote or wrote almost all of them! She cowrote "Please Please Please" and "Espresso" with songwriter Amy Allen, whom she describes as a "once-in-a-lifetime writer and friend".

What was the set design for Sabrina's Short n' Sweet tour?

---

a) A giant dollhouse

b) A coffee shop

c) A hair salon

Whatever is meant for you will find you effortlessly.

SABRINA CARPENTER

# DID YOU KNOW...

Sabrina's green flag when it comes to songs is writing honest lyrics. For touring, her green flags are getting enough sleep, being present when performing and having lots of fun with the crowd. In dating, her green flags are consistency, communication and a date that takes care of their own well-being.

Sabrina is proud to be short of stature, and her 2024 album title even points to her height. What is her actual measurement?

———

a) 5 ft

b) 5.5 ft

c) 4.5 ft

# I WANT TO BE HONEST —

# I WANT TO JUST WRITE ABOUT WHAT'S HAPPENING IN MY LIFE.

SABRINA CARPENTER

# DID YOU KNOW...

To reveal the title of her new song "Vicious" in 2022, Sabrina made a Spotify playlist with seven songs, each beginning with one of the letters in "Vicious". The songs included "Vienna" by Billy Joel, "I Hate U" by SZA, "Cigarette Daydreams" by Cage the Elephant and "I Gotta Feeling" by the Black Eyed Peas.

Which of Sabrina's friends stars with her in the music video for "Sue Me"?

---

a) Dove Cameron

b) Joey King

c) Taylor Swift

FOCUS ON THE
POSITIVE AND
KNOW THERE ARE
SO MANY PEOPLE
AROUND YOU
THAT LOVE YOU.

SABRINA CARPENTER

# DID YOU KNOW...

Sabrina prioritizes self-care. She practises gratitude by listing things she is thankful for when she wakes every morning, setting herself up for the rest of the day. She also looks after her inner peace by taking regular baths to de-stress and uses essential oils through a diffuser to help energize her when she has early morning starts.

How many outfits does
Sabrina have in the
"Fast Times" music video?

———

a) Four

b) Five

c) Six

Femininity is something that I've always embraced.

SABRINA CARPENTER

# DID YOU KNOW...

On the Short n' Sweet tour, for the song "Juno", Sabrina picked someone to be arrested with pink handcuffs on the side of the stage for being "too hot". On one of the London dates, Spice Girl member Emma Bunton was chosen, and Sabrina personalized the moment to honour Emma by exclaiming, "You're kinda, like, spicing up my life a little."

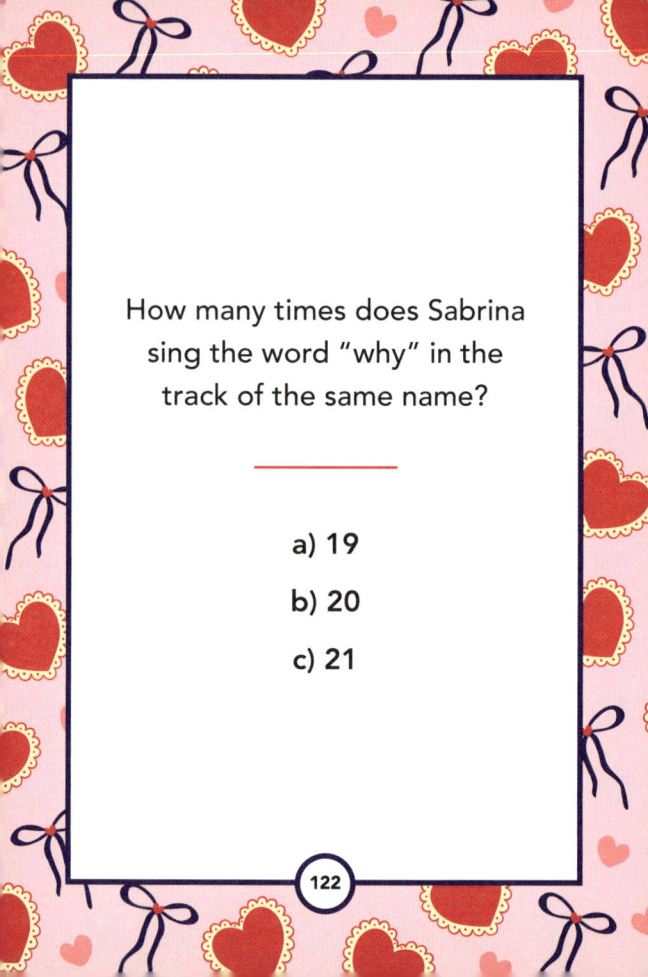

How many times does Sabrina sing the word "why" in the track of the same name?

a) 19
b) 20
c) 21

# IT'S A LOT MORE FREEING

# TO JUST BE YOURSELF.

SABRINA CARPENTER

# DID YOU KNOW...

At the start of the song "Espresso" on each night of her Short n' Sweet tour, Sabrina rose up from under the stage with a steaming mug of what looked like espresso. Every city of the tour had a personalized mug with the name of the city and her signature red lipstick stain printed on it.

The name of which band is featured on the top Sabrina's character wears in her first appearance on *Girl Meets World*?

---

a) AC/DC

b) Pink Floyd

c) The Beatles

There's a really good chance that no one's paying attention to the things that you're so focused on. People just see you for the best parts of yourself.

SABRINA CARPENTER

# DID YOU KNOW...

Sabrina is super flexible! She can do a cartwheel, the splits and even a round-off tumble. These amazing gymnastics skills have come in handy when performing the song "Juno" onstage – at one show she went into a crab pose and at another she did the splits!

Which of these films does Sabrina star in alongside Amandla Stenberg and KJ Apa?

---

a) *Tall Girl*
b) *The Hate You Give*
c) *Clouds*

*Writing music has been my self-care.*

SABRINA CARPENTER

# DID YOU KNOW...

When Sabrina experienced heartbreak for the first time, she felt she had to do something to make herself feel better. She decided a new haircut was the way to go and cut herself her signature bangs. The singer later explained that she isn't usually one to make sudden spontaneous decisions, but the overwhelming feelings of heartbreak made her want to make a change and do something different!

How many songs in total make up Acts I and II of Sabrina's two-part studio album project *Singular*?

---

a) 16
b) 17
c) 18

**I'VE ALWAYS YEARNED TO CARE ENOUGH ABOUT A PERSON OR A**

**SITUATION OR A RELATIONSHIP IN MY LIFE THAT IT PROVOKES THAT MUCH FEELING IN ME.**

SABRINA CARPENTER

# DID YOU KNOW...

In 2024, a video of Sabrina as a child talking to her cat resurfaced and went viral. After joking that she went to animal communication school, young Sabrina says "Meow. Purr. Hiss" to her cat. She then exclaims, "He's intimidated. You see that intimidation in his eyes?" Fans have said the video captures Sabrina's humorous side.

Sabrina has admitted to feeling starstruck when she met a celebrity. Which of these stars was she referring to?

———

a) Lin-Manuel Miranda

b) Angelina Jolie

c) Hugh Jackman

> THERE ARE SO MANY TIMES IN LIFE WHERE WE'RE FOCUSED ON SOMETHING ELSE THAT WE'RE MISSING WHAT'S RIGHT IN FRONT OF US.

SABRINA CARPENTER

# DID YOU KNOW...

The album that inspired Sabrina to write more freely for *Short n' Sweet* was *Lemonade* by Beyoncé. *Lemonade* is experimental and crosses boundaries in terms of genre. Listening to it helped Sabrina go ahead and write what she wanted to, rather than trying to get her music to fit a certain genre.

In which of these settings has Sabrina not done an interview?

---

a) A ball pit

b) Among puppies

c) Sat on a swimming pool inflatable

I never want to be too comfortable in what I'm doing. I always wanna be afraid and nervous and excited.

SABRINA CARPENTER

# DID YOU KNOW...

Sabrina Carpenter's go-to hot drink isn't actually an espresso as some might think. She instead has an obsession with an Argentinian tea made from yerba mate leaves. The herbal infusion is thought to have several health benefits, including being full of antioxidants, and is said to increase energy levels.

What brand of mascara did Sabrina headline the campaign for in 2025?

---

a) Prada
b) Dior
c) YSL

# LOVE IS SOMETHING YOU

# DON'T HAVE TO QUESTION; YOU JUST FEEL IT.

SABRINA CARPENTER

# DID YOU KNOW...

Sabrina chose the title *Singular* for her third and fourth studio albums because, once she had written all the songs and listened to them again, the overarching theme was an "unspoken confidence". She felt the title *Singular* was the perfect name to relay this theme.

How long did it take Sabrina initially to write "Espresso"?

---

a) 30 minutes

b) 1 hour

c) 1 week

LIFE DOESN'T STOP, SO IT'S REALLY HARD TO TELL WHEN A CHAPTER OF YOUR LIFE SHOULD BE BOOKENDED.

SABRINA CARPENTER

# DID YOU KNOW...

Sabrina's parents, Elizabeth and David, have always been very supportive of her creative ambitions. Her mum was a dancer and her dad was in a garage band, so they both had experience of performing. Her dad even built her a recording studio when she was just ten years old in the closet of their house!

What was Sabrina's Netflix 2024 Christmas special called?

a) *An Espresso Christmas*

b) *A Nonsense Christmas*

c) *A Short n' Sweet Christmas*

The music that I make is a huge part of the person that I am.

SABRINA CARPENTER

# DID YOU KNOW...

Sabrina wrote *emails i can't send* as a heartbreak album, hence the raw front cover image of her in a black dress sat with a computer. Her look was inspired by old photos of Kate Moss. It gives off an isolated feel, with Sabrina's back turned away from the camera, and the simplicity of it has a timeless quality. She says this album, and especially the tour attached to it, helped her evolve into her *Short n' Sweet* era.

In the first line of "skinny dipping", on which day of the week does the speaker say she'll be in a coffee shop?

———

a) Monday

b) Tuesday

c) Wednesday

# I JUST DON'T WANT TO LIVE OUT OF FEAR,

# TRYING TO MAKE SURE I DON'T UPSET ANYONE.

SABRINA CARPENTER

# DID YOU KNOW...

When Sabrina starts dating someone, she likes to know if they have friends they've been close to for most of their life. She believes having this type of connection says a lot about a person because life-long friends keep you grounded.

Who designed Sabrina's 2025 Met Gala look?

---

a) Alexander McQueen

b) Marc Jacobs

c) Pharrell Williams for Louis Vuitton

KEEP BELIEVING
IN YOURSELVES
AND DREAM.

SABRINA CARPENTER

# DID YOU KNOW...

Sabrina has always been a fan of Christina Aguilera, and she covered her song "Oh Mother" back in 2010 on her YouTube channel. She wouldn't have believed then that in September 2024 she would get the chance to perform and record a reimagined version of "What a Girl Wants" with Christina for the 25th anniversary of Christina Aguilera's self-titled album. What a full-circle moment!

Which European city is also a song title on *Singular: Act I*?

---

a) Paris

b) Rome

c) Barcelona

Whatever's in the past, keep it in the past. Look forward and look at all the great things in your life.

SABRINA CARPENTER

# FINAL WORD

Now you've listened to these short n' sweet words of wisdom from the princess of pop and learned how to embrace your unique personality and find your creative spark, you're ready to be your most confident self and take on the world!

Return to this book any time you need a pocket-sized pick-me-up – Sabrina's life lessons truly are the blueprint for living your no-nonsense best life!

# ANSWERS

8. a
11. b
14. b
17. c
20. b
23. a
26. a
29. a
32. c
35. c
38. b
41. c
44. a

47. a
50. c
53. a
56. b
59. c
62. a
65. c
68. a
71. b
74. b
77. a
80. b
83. a

| | |
|---|---|
| 86. a | 122. c |
| 89. b | 125. a |
| 92. c | 128. b |
| 95. c | 131. b |
| 98. a | 134. a |
| 101. a | 137. c |
| 104. c | 140. a |
| 107. c | 143. a |
| 110. a | 146. b |
| 113. a | 149. c |
| 116. b | 152. c |
| 119. b | 155. a |

Have you enjoyed this book? If so, find us on Facebook at **Summersdale Publishers**, on Twitter/X at **@Summersdale** and on Instagram, TikTok and Bluesky at **@summersdalebooks** and get in touch. We'd love to hear from you!

**www.summersdale.com**

## IMAGE CREDITS

p.3 and throughout – bow © tanyabosyk/Shutterstock.com; p.5 and p.157 – microphone © Tartila/Shutterstock.com; p.6 and throughout – guitar © Quang Vinh Tran/Shutterstock.com; p.8 and throughout – bows © Eyshilaa/Shutterstock.com, hearts © cloverlittleworld/Shutterstock.com; p.12 and throughout – lips © Nadya_Art/Shutterstock.com; p.21 and throughout – boot © MyPro/Shutterstock.com

86. a
89. b
92. c
95. c
98. a
101. a
104. c
107. c
110. a
113. a
116. b
119. b

122. c
125. a
128. b
131. b
134. a
137. c
140. a
143. a
146. b
149. c
152. c
155. a

Have you enjoyed this book? If so, find us on Facebook at **Summersdale Publishers**, on Twitter/X at **@Summersdale** and on Instagram, TikTok and Bluesky at **@summersdalebooks** and get in touch. We'd love to hear from you!

**www.summersdale.com**

## IMAGE CREDITS

p.3 and throughout – bow © tanyabosyk/Shutterstock.com; p.5 and p.157 – microphone © Tartila/Shutterstock.com; p.6 and throughout – guitar © Quang Vinh Tran/Shutterstock.com; p.8 and throughout – bows © Eyshilaa/Shutterstock.com, hearts © cloverlittleworld/Shutterstock.com; p.12 and throughout – lips © Nadya_Art/Shutterstock.com; p.21 and throughout – boot © MyPro/Shutterstock.com